T0197248

The
Invisible Scars

The
Invisible Scars

HILMI I. MAVIOGLU

THE INVISIBLE SCARS

Copyright © 2018 Hilmi I. Mavioglu.

All rights reserved. No part of this book may be used or reproduced by any means, graphic, electronic, or mechanical, including photocopying, recording, taping or by any information storage retrieval system without the written permission of the author except in the case of brief quotations embodied in critical articles and reviews.

iUniverse books may be ordered through booksellers or by contacting:

iUniverse
1663 Liberty Drive
Bloomington, IN 47403
www.iuniverse.com
1-800-Authors (1-800-288-4677)

Because of the dynamic nature of the Internet, any web addresses or links contained in this book may have changed since publication and may no longer be valid. The views expressed in this work are solely those of the author and do not necessarily reflect the views of the publisher, and the publisher hereby disclaims any responsibility for them.

Any people depicted in stock imagery provided by Getty Images are models, and such images are being used for illustrative purposes only. Certain stock imagery © Getty Images.

ISBN: 978-1-5320-5119-7 (sc)
ISBN: 978-1-5320-5120-3 (e)

Print information available on the last page.

iUniverse rev. date: 06/15/2018

Acknowledgement

This is my fourth book of epic poems. This book's characters, historical events and geographical locations are fictitious; they may be parallel to reality, whereas they are not of reality, itself.

I am grateful for many places that I have been, and the many souls I have met.

These poems came to me at their chosen moments, and I celebrated their birth with the following kindred spirits: Suzan Barnes, Christa Richardson, Kirk Firestone, Dr. Nickleby Bashö, and Joyce, Neslihan and Kurt Mavioglu.

From Spokane to the Lake Pend Oreille

Ivana told her husband, Emil,
That today we were to visit with Konyas.

However, last night's torrential rain may
Have washed out a segment of the dirt road.

Since Konyas have no phone in their beach house,
I can't find out what actually has happened.

I'm not making a big deal out of this,
Yet it's not an easy task to cancel
A visit with them and reschedule it.
Konyas' lifestyle is not flexible.

They travel and live in many countries.
I wonder how they could find new places
To visit, for they've already seen many
Places on this planet Earth, exotic or not.

As a result of their past experiences,
They never go to a particular old country.

Just to change the topic of conversation,
Emil said, "Anytime of the year is
A good time to visit the North Idaho."

On that hot day, they left Spokane early.
Allowing extra time for themselves,

In case any major washout took place
On the last dirt segment of the road,
Which ends at Konyas' lakeside property.

The road from Spokane to Bayview was standard.
For them there was nothing new to behold.

In spite of that, all things looked fresh and new,
As if they were passing that exotic
Scenery for the first time in their lives.

Under the bright sun even the standard
Highway signs for the lakes appeared alluring:
Liberty, Coeur d'Alene, Twin, Spirit, Pend
Oreille, Grant, Kelso, Cocolalla,
Hauser, Hayden, Hoodoo and on and on.

Emil's Mind was Searching

By the time they reached Rathdrum Prairie,
Emil's mind was pulsating, chanting and
Casting exotic spells on itself like
The mind of a Pend Oreille medicine man:
Hauser, Haden, d Hoodoo, Hoodoo, Hoodoo...

The time telescoped on itself so that
The artificial division of time
Lost its distinction. The past, the present
And the future spliced on each other
To form a unit as it ought to be:
Without a beginning or an ending.

Emil imagined that the Earth wobbled on
Its axis and started to look cockeyed
At the Sun thus received less energy.

Soon after that the Earth started to shudder;
Yet the sun was emitting as always.

The Continental thick ice sheets started
To march from the British Columbia
On the way to south through the Purcell Trench.

What could flee did flee towards the warmer air.
What could not flee was crushed by the ice sheets.

Season after season as the ice crept
South, it smothered the Earth and dug the ground.

One kind of brutal force was pitted against
Another kind so that they'd tamed each other.

The Columbia River

For thousands of years the main channel
Of the Columbia River cascaded
Through the present day Highway Forty-one.

Once again the powerful river reclaimed
Its original northerly channel.
Finally, North Idaho healed herself.

Panhandle of Idaho

Once more, pine forests covered Idaho's face,
Only yesterday the towns and fields claimed
Small patches of land from the forests,
Still pines thrive at their doorsteps and scent their homes.

Folks say, "Under the calm surface, there reigns
A rabid ghost which resides in Spirit Lake,
And funnels through the trusty Purcell Trench."

To prove their claim, they point out the presence
Of racists, religious extremists and cults,
And the existence of devil worshippers.

Actually those folks are young and they need
Time to grow up and be toned down by time.

Fish Tales

The smell of syringa sobered Emil.
He started to talk about several
Fishing trips that he took in the Lake Pend Oreille.

His tale was unchanging at one aspect:
The weight of Kamloops Rainbow Trout of the Clark
Fork River would not be less than thirty five pounds.

Bayview

They turned east at Athol and went across
The Farragut State Park. When the road was
Winding down, they noticed the bright blue eyes
Of the Scenic Bay which was luring them
To come closer to the village of Bayview,
Which is not as yet parceled and polished
For the rich; so she still keeps her beauty.

Past Bayview they found the familiar dirt
Road which was extending towards eastward.
To the north of the lake, the appearance
Turned harsh and it looked like rock quarry.
Dirt road was Just like a single spider silk.

The road had no regular highway signs;
Although it had its unmistakable markers.

To the south, the lake was painted in shades of blues.
Closer to the shore the lake was aqua.
Closer to the shallows it was turquoise.
At the center it would turn deep navy.

When the skies of the lake turns overcast,
Then the color of the lake turns cobalt blue.

The road like that could not have been no other
Road than the road that leads to the Konyas' estate.

Emil was watching the ruts in the road,
And they themselves were being observed
By a curious flock of mountain goats,
Which were perching up on the lofty cliffs.

When the road was ended on a hilly
Meadow, Emil was sure that they arrived
Konyas' Lake Pend Oreille property.

The Blockhouse

On a hillock a pioneer built blockhouse
Was standing as if it was built yesterday.

The trees around the blockhouse are the same age.
It is obvious that the trees were removed,
So that no one could sneak up to the blockhouse.

When the security was no longer
A vital concern, they let the trees grow again.

The foundation of the blockhouse was dug
Deep down to the granite bedrock,
And they were raised two feet above the ground.

On the south side the granite blocks were bleached by
The sun and they were kept clean by the rains.
On the north side they were covered with moss.

To build the blockhouse chosen cedar logs
Were hewn and fitted so skillfully that
Even today one can't slip a single
Layer of paper between those old logs.

On the north side there was a narrow stairway
Which was leading to a well fitted door,
And behind that door a root cellar was hidden
To keep their potatoes fresh all year round.

The Property

The property is spread on the side of
A hill and covered by a cedar grove.

A few acres around the cabin were
Cleared of its ancient cedars to offer
A little breathing room for the fruit trees,
So that they could fully mature and provide.

The lawn was a common ground for the green
Living things which did not mind to be moved.

For the Konyas any grass was welcome,
Whether it was Bermuda or Witch Grass.

Clover was allowed to grow on the lawn,
And the dandelions were not ostracized.
Their yellow bonnets raised no one's eyebrows.

The Potato Patch

The potato patch was chosen and catered to,
And it was expected to produce well.
There, no evergreens were allowed to cast
Their shadows, or shed their needles upon it.

No weed could creep or trespass on that patch
Without being caught and executed.

The patch was shaped as a geometrically
Correct square to receive direct sunlight.
So that the potato plants can flourish.

Straight rows had enough distance from each other,
So the dark green leaves were free to capture
The sun's energy to sustain their growth.

This couple knew and understood the basic
Facts of life forms as the ancient Aztecs
And Egyptians knew and set their calendars
As to when to plant and when to harvest.

The potato patch was their calendar.
The changes of the texture of its soil,
Under the spring sun, guides them as to when
To travel and when to come back to plant.

There was a good size orchard near the beach,
But it was not clear as to who owned it.

Each Fall, bears would come and harvest the fruits,
And in the process they'd damage the trees,
And they'd love to punish the apple trees.

Arpad would mend the trees every spring
As if he were in an operating room.
Amputating some severely damaged
Limbs and splinting the less injured ones.

Ritual Fire

Noticing the scorched bark of a yellow
Pine and a pile of fresh ashes and cinders,
Emil asked, "How close was that soul to you?"
Arpad said, "A friend whose space can't be filled."

Though, Emil knows that Arpad calls himself
"A pagan at Heart, and" when he loses
A friend, he builds a fire for the memories
Of the deceased, since fire purifies all.

The Silver Creek

At the bottom of the hill, just behind
The blockhouse, there is a stream that bubbles through
The ground which feels cool during the summer
And steaming warm during the winter.

Birds and animals preferred to drink, from the creek,
Just before it's diluted with the lake water.

After the birds' migration to the south,
The creek won't go silent; it will sound deeper.

Bull Elk

Bull elks come in October by bugling
To announce that it is rutting time.
And they are ready to batter anyone
Who happened to be just in their way.

The Beach House

When the Konyas bought the beach front property,
They locked up the old blockhouse and hired an
Architect to reconstruct the blockhouse,
And also build a new modern residence.

Anticipating the arrival of
Their guests, Konyas unlocked the outer gate.
Then they lounged next to the potato patch

When the guests came, Eva moved towards them
So nimbly that on her path neither the
Air was cleaved nor a blade of grass was bruised.

Arpad moved like an M1A2 Abrams tank.
Its rusty road wheels softly squeaked and creaked,
And yet its old brakes could stop on a dime.

Their Kuvasz still acted like a puppy
But his rippling muscles beneath his wavy
White coat gave away his actual age.

For generations, kuvasz breed of dogs
Guarded the castle of the Hungarian kings,
And protected the flocks of the shepherds.

After they moved inside, their conversation
Gradually shifted to the traveling.

Konyas' Visit to Tibet

Recently they visited Tibet.
Where the old temples were shut down and most
Of the old monks were displaced and silenced,

Yet today's Chinese soldiers will not be
Able to stop tomorrow's whisperings
For freedom, which will get louder by each
Passing moments. Yet Chinese will not hear,
And at last they'll assimilate Tibet,
No doubts, it is just a matter of time.

Konyas don't pass judgment on outwardly fate
Of the people. No word about the poor
Living conditions of the common folks.

Konyas don't go around to collect negative
Information about the distant places.

Arpad Read Words from the Tibeto-Burman

Arpad pulled out his notebook and began
To read out loud a few words from the Tibetan,
And other languages which were referring
To daily living and natural events.

He analyzed each word from several
Present day languages for likenesses.
He said, "Mother tongues come from the same roots."

His hypothesis have not been accepted.
Yet it is not dampening his enthusiasm.

For years Arpad has been studying runic,
And pictographic writings of the Indians.

He thinks that there is a basic connection
Between writings of different cultures,

He considers pictography as
A form of writing and he's an expert in it.
He's focusing his energy on them.

The Lake Pend Oreille

Whoever lives at the shores of this restless
Lake must have a boat, for many places
Can be reached only by water transportation.

Present day dirt roads are a luxury.
When the blockhouse was being built, there were no roads.

Arpad's boat is a rebuilt motorboat.
It is mostly used for recreation.
Also it'll reach places faster on the lake.

His boat is used for mystical ways too,
And it's decorated accordingly.

A thunderbird is painted on each side.
Their colors are washed and faded and yet
Basic pigments are still vivid enough
To suggest that those thunderbirds might flap
Their wings and cause the heavens to roar.
A bunch of eager to fly eagle feathers
Are hanging loose from a pole at its bow.

There are blue sacks which are beaded with blue
Beads and filled with sun dried white Syringa
Flowers and hung on the walls of the cabin.

Cruising the Lake

When they were all aboard, they headed north.
Arpad said, "Adoring this lake is not
Enough; it also deserves to be loved."

It is shaped just like a big question mark.
And it is still a mystery as to
How it might have been formed at that location.

Creation of the Lake Pend Oreille According to Indians

"I'd like to believe as it is explained
In the Pend Oreille Indians legends.

"Many moons ago, when the Mother Earth
And the Moon were so young that their faces
Were as smooth as the bark of a young birch,

"They led such a leisurely and joyous
Lifestyle that it was unlikely for them
To develop deep wrinkles and pockmarks.

"One day Mother Earth developed a fever,
And a bellyache which got worse quickly,
And her abdomen swelled and rumbled so
Loud that the Great Spirit heard it and extended
His hand and touched on the swollen area.

"A channel was opened for her burning
Blood to gush out and to relieve her distress.

"Spilled blood into the lake lost its pigment,
Her plasma oozed and pooled to form this lake.

The Spirit of the Depths took residence
And started to dig deeper and deeper.
That's why there is no bottom to this lake.

"While Mother Earth was caring for her children,
The lake developed a chill which was coming
From the environment and hurting her being.
Her skin was scraped and wrinkled by the ice.

"At the Pend Oreille Trench, ice had to fight
With granites, and it was a well matched fight.

As the ice pounded the granite skeleton
Of the lake, the ice sheet was tamed and confined
By the granite, though the water turned milky
For some time; then it turned sky blue."

The Spirit of the Depths

Indians believed in the Spirit of the Depths,
Before they'd get into their dugout canoes,
They checked to be sure that they had enough
Syringa as a protective medicine.

When the lake grows angry and starts to foam,
Only Syringa flowers would please the Spirit
Of the Depths, and she would turn the angry
White waters back to reassuring blue.

When the lonely spirit feels frolicsome,
She'll let the phosphorescence of the water
Give an appearance to the lake, as if
Her surface is covered with a gold foil,
Which is free to ripple and wrinkle.

Many Moods of the Lake

Emil said, Most people think that this lake
Is too rough, too deep, too cold, too untamed
Or too something else, and yet they love her.

Arpad continued, this lake is what it is.
Here the nature is in perfect balance.

When the waves get to rough and pound the shores
With fury, then the granites of the shores
Spit the waves right back where they are belong;
Nothing is ruined, nothing is washed out.

As the early fall snow begins to fall,
And keep falling, layer upon layer,
Evergreens turn into mini pyramids
Which reveal only a hint of green streaks.

And the silence layers upon silence.
It grows so quiet that one can hear the clicking
Of his thoughts falling into their right slots,
And yet stray irrational thoughts interfere.

To his surprise, one finds oneself asking,
"Shall that snow ever melt?" or "Is this just
A beginning of another Ice Age?"

When the spring Chinook Winds start to blow,
It may feel cool enough to chill our bones.
But for the accumulated snow it is
Hotter than the fiery breath of a dragon.

The Spring Runoff

As the winter takes off its white garment,
Spring runoff hurries down clear and clean,
For it is filtered by the undergrowth.

What spills over the steep shores is a pure
And irreplaceable sustainer of life.

The Summer Sun

When the hot summer sun smiles to the lake,
She'll grab as much energy as she can,
And starts to wear a warm smile to entice
The people to jump in, yet one must
Be a grateful guest and do not make waves.

Otherwise cold water hiding just beneath
The surface hits him on the back to remind
Him that, when one is dealing with this lake,
There are boundaries that one must respect.

The Clark Fork River and the Missoula Lake

He turned east and navigated into
The estuary of the Clark Fork River,
Soon after the canyon became narrower,
And the flow of the river grew stronger
To remind us that what was seen and felt
Today can't be compared to what has happened.
Clar k Fork River Carried water
As the rivers of today put together.
When the Ice Age Missoula Lake broke through.
The Cabinet Gorge for a few days,
The Clark Fork River is carried more water
Then all of the rivers of today put together.
And as free as any river of our time.
At any time of the year it winds through
The plains, speeding through the narrowest canyons,
Cascades over the falls, foams, and quiets down.

When the Ice Age
Missoula Lake Broke

Through, the Cabinet Gorge, for a few days,
The Clark Fork river carried more water
Then all of the rivers of today put together.

Healing Flood Story

Every culture has a vague flood story.
Only this flood has supporting data.

In Pend Oreille Indian dialect
"Missoula" translates to "freezing water."

We have seen the scablands of the Eastern
Washington, stretching from Vantage to Spokane;
The terrain is scrubbed clean of top soil.

Ancient river channels crisscross each other
Without a trickle of water in them,
And the present day rivers run far below.

The Clark Fork River already reached its zenith,
Found its soul and left its mark on the land.

Nowadays what Clark Fork River might do
Or might not do is just a guessing game.

Arpod turned his boat towards the west and
Gunned the engine towards the Sandpoint.

He pointed at the Memaloose Island
And said, "I'd like to make a pilgrimage
To that island to visit with the souls there."

They left the boat at the Clear Creek Marina.
Then they went to the Floating Restaurant.

Emil's nice Isabella was there waiting.
Introductions were over in no time,
And they went over the daily news quickly.

Then Isabella started to talk about
The recent international politics.

She expressed her surprise regarding
The disintegration of the eastern

Block countries and inquired if Konyas would
Ever consider visiting the Hungary.

The Hungary in Cold War Time

Arpad said, "Yes, In the old countries governments
May crumble, just like an eggshell, but no
One can be sure as to what shall be hatched."

"We dealt with communists for the last sixty years,
But we had been dealing with Russian
And Slavic nationalism for centuries.
I'd say, the old snake is shedding its skin."

Eva Talked About Her Whipping

Eva started to talk and tried to control
The tears which were rolling down on her cheeks.
Almost in a softest whisper, she said,
"I was whipped by a young Russian soldier."

Ivana Tried to Change the Topic

Ivana attempted to change the topic
Of conversation by talking about
The high quality of the food and drinks.

Surely, she knew how unpleasant memories
And invisible scars can haunt and hurt.

Arpad Recited a Poem

Arpad said, "A Hungarian poet's
Poem, pertaining to going back home,
Is constantly echoing in my mind.
If you don't mind, I would like to recite it."

"One may go though, one may not return.
One may return back, though one may not find.

While dreaming of back home, I start to fantasize.
The cinders of the past flare up, I realize.
Going back and presenting myself is easy.
So who's there to notice? Who's there to recognize?"

Everything Recycles

In this universe all things do recycle.
What may appear to us as the decay
Or evil may be due to false observations.

We see merely the veneer when we visit
With other people. We must be contented
For we can observe their outwardly beliefs.

We must be satisfied with what we could
Catch with one short click of the camera.
Life is fleeting moments of joy or sadness.

The growth and the decay follow each other.
We won't grow towards the same direction.
The space between people widen as they age.

Isabella Plans to Have an Interview with the Konyas

After a delightful evening they went home.
The next evening Isabella stated
Her intention to her uncle Emil.

She planned to have an interview with the Konyas,
And after going over it, she'd like
To have more information to refine
It into an article to publish
In the newspaper where she is employed.

Emil said, "You can't obtain their consent,
Or cooperation to make it easy.

Your journalistic approaches won't work.
They won't let you expose their private world."

"You should approach this undertaking,
As if it were a long-term project.

You can't ask questions and write down the answers.
Their story did not happen in one day.
So that, you can't have it all in one day.

In this case, you must listen and decipher,
And eventually be satisfied with
What you have, for no true tale is endless."

Emile is Asked to Facilitate

Isabella said to Emil, "You may
Help for you too lived in diverse countries."
Emil, "Yes and no, for people's lives can
Be parallel, yet they won't overlap."

"Yes, we too lived in different countries,
And confronted with many different cultures.
We untangled our problems like a child.

We held on to the skirt of the Mother Land,
And made sure that our passports were valid.

After being firmly established in
This land, still the mother land stayed in our hearts."

Konyas' Circumstances

Konyas' circumstances were different.
They were not trying to go to a new
Country to have better opportunities,
On the contrary, they were escaping
From the country that they loved and cherished.

To get out of the Hungary, they've risked
All they have had: their homeland, their marriage,
Their lives, and their standing in their country.

For them, going back home was not an option,
So, without hesitation, they burned their bridges.

Long Years of Friendship

During our long years of friendship, they talked
As they felt like it; and we just listened;
No questioning; when the knives of the past
Started to cut into the living flesh
Of the present, we tried to grind the sharp edges
Of the salt crystals of the pickled past.
We heard the silence in between the lines,
And that silence told the true story.

The true story is not what is revealed,
But what's shined back from the screen of the past."

Arpad's Past

Arpad was born in the Marosvasarhely
In Transylvania when that country
Was an integral part of the Hungary.

His father was a history teacher,
And an experienced interpreter
Of the runic poems of the Hungarians.
His mother was a high school French teacher.

When Arpad was old enough not to forget,
Transylvania was annexed to the Romania.

Before he was old enough to master
Swimming in the cool waters of the Maros
River, his family moved to Szeged,
At the junction of the Maros and Tisza rivers.

To make Arpad secure in his new realm,
His father used to say, "We did not lose
A river, but we found another one."
Yet Arpad did not feel like finding anything.

The Maros river was not the same river:
She was diminished, shallow, and became
Subservient, when she joined with the Tisza.
She changed her name and lost her identity.

He saw the Tisza river as a big
Monster which swallows its young ones
To grow uglier; he did not swim in it.

During the cold nights of Szeged, they would
Sit around the fireplace, and his mother
Would read half forgotten Magyar epics.

Adaptation

With each passing year, the echoes of
The past sounded more and more distant.
Just the demands of daily living
Left no leisure time for nostalgia.

When a tree is planted, even in a
Fertile soil, it will still have an initial
Period of shock, then it will catch up.

Arpad dove into the mainstream of life.
And the life smiled back; he excelled in school,
Both academically and in sports.
It was smooth sailing, no choppiness.

Graduation From the Medical School

He graduated from medical school
And started his surgical residency.

Noticing a Girl

He noticed a freshman medical school
Student, who was gracefully gliding
Over the stairs, nothing like he'd seen before,
And then that perfect figure passed him by.

He made no attempt to get to know her,
For years of studies were ahead of him.
He saw her as someone who could change his plans,
And he was not ready to give a chance
To anyone to alter his long-term goals.

Yet, not running toward her did not mean
Running away from her charm and attraction.

Day by day, he watched her in the classrooms,
The hallways, the cafeteria and the library.

Each time he was discovering one
More hidden delicate feature of hers
That he could not appreciate before.

He realized that he could no longer
Escape from what the fate had in store for him.

When she was having a cup of coffee,
Arpad neared and asked if he could join her?
A crystal clear voice simply said "Yes, please".

It was one of those moments that simple
Words come with unintentional meanings.

Her words were fluid without a freezing point.
And they were flowing smoothly with soft ripples.

She said her name was Eva and she was
A freshman and continued, "I still have
Not adjusted to the campus life in a
Cosmopolitan city like Budapest.

As you know better than I do, soon hard
Work will catch up with us and we will have
No time to think about daily events."
It felt good to talk without being complex.

They started to synchronize their coffee brakes.
When their plans did not let them do so,
They felt like they were missing something important.

Whenever Eva was getting ready
For an examination, Arpad groomed
Her as to what topics she should concentrate on.

Eva is Helping Arpad

One day, Arpad casually mentioned that
To strengthen his thesis, he needed to have
Access to the French medical literature.

He needed to know someone who could translate
Certain important research articles.

Eva said, "Look no further than this table.
I can translate them as we sip our coffees."

Eva's grandmother was a French lady,
Eva used to enjoy some of her summer
Vacations in France with her relatives.

Those translation sessions became a joy
For both of them, especially for Arpad.

As she read aloud the French articles,
And as she rolled her R's, she pursed her lips
As if she were ready to give a French kiss.

Eva and Arpad are Getting Romantic

When Arpad thanked her for the help he received,
They gazed deep into each other's eyes
Both of them saw their reflection in the
Eyes of the other one which sealed their destinies.

Looking to the Future Together

The scholastic year went well for both of them:
Eva were to start her advanced studies.
Arpad were to finish his residency,
Pass his surgical board examination,
And begin his academic career,
And they were to seal their loves to each other,

And they were to get married with body
And soul, and it were to last a lifetime.

Honeymoon in Transylvania

The Transylvania once more became
A subdivision of the Hungary,
Since Transylvania was Arpad's birthplace
They wanted have their honeymoon there.

The World War II

We make plans and the life modifies them,
Also eternal clock of time keeps ticking.
What they did not plan for was the World War II.

Arpad was Drafted

Arpad was drafted into military,
And ordered to report in seven days.
There was no certainty of coming back.
There was no prospect of luminous days.

The Wedding Had to be Done

The wedding had to be done then and there.
They had no time to spend on ceremonies.
They exchanged their wedding vows, just their way.

The war not only kills and maims people,
It also turns their dreams into nightmares
By disrupting the normal flow of life.

The Military Wants to Have Physicians as Soon as Possible

They told Eva's class that their country
Demands more young physicians to serve her.
To achieve that goal, they were to study
Harder to receive their MD degrees
Sooner than during peace time training.

That did not work for the students spent more
Time in bomb shelters than the classrooms.

Eva realized that she could not get
Her MD degree during war times.

The World War II was Over Without Peace in the Country

The World War II was over; however,
There was no sign of peace in Hungary.
She was occupied by the Communists.

During her long history, Hungary
Had many defeats and victories.
Each time people were able to bounce back.

Tough, this time it looked as if life was
In a wrong channel, and it was flowing
Towards a most sinistrous direction.

Bards of Ancient Magyars

Arpad recalled the epics that his mother
Used to read when he was a youngster.

When the ancient Magyars had a setback,
The bards would start the healing process by
Singing the songs of glorious old days,
And their last song would be dedicated
To the happy days which were soon to arrive.

Coming of Communism

This time no one was daring to whisper,
Much less to think or open their sealed mouths.
Folks were stunned with changes that were taking place.

A New Class of People

When the Communists came to power with
The backing of Russia, they created
A new class of power hungry bloodsuckers.

They demanded that the old people should
Keep their mouth shut and use it just to eat.
For them knowing the old ways was a crime.

Folk's brains were to be used to learn instructions
Which were approved by the Communist Party.

One should not waste his time by thinking about
Old ideas that were proven to be wrong.

And any idea which was not approved
By the Communist Party was unsound.

People's words were to be used to help
The officials to erase the old ways.

Those who could not fit to today would not be
Saved for the future, for it would be a waste
Of time to rehabilitate that group.

Fast and Slow Learners

The Communist Party recognized that some
Were fast learners, and some were slow learners.
They let the fast learners teach the slow learners.

Teaching of a Slow Learner

Communist agents determined that a
Certain young physician was a slow learner.
So he was in need of help in a proper place.

He was arrested without any charges,
And shoved into the holding cell of a jail.

That place was packed with people who left no
Room to sit down, much less to catch some sleep.

Since there was no place to clean themselves,
People stunk badly due to body odor.

It's said that the body odor of people
Is just as bad as the sprays of skunks,
Which helped for the survival of our species.
Predators did not want to go near them.

The holding cell was nothing like he dreamt,
It could have been a weight reduction spa.

Though food was meager, and there was no cook or server.

One could eat as much as he wanted,
If one could stand the taste and the smell of it.

The flow of time changed so that he was not
Sure whether it was too slow or too fast.

A Visit for Arpad by an Agent

One day a young agent paid a visit.
He carried out a light conversation.

Then casually asked the doctor if he
Would like to take a leisurely shower.

The doctor accepted his kindly offer
Even though he had no clean clothes to wear.

The Doctor Tried to Guess what Kind of a Person that Agent was ....

In his mind doctor tried to guess the social
Standing of that agent and decided
That he was a normal Hungarian.
His handsome face was trusting and innocent.
He could have been one of doctor's nephews,
Or any young member of his family.

As the agent let him go through a hallway,
The doctor kept observing the agent,
Who appeared well seasoned beyond his years,
And the basic gentleness was not lacking.

The Doctor's Face was Slapped with the Cold Air of the Room

When they entered into a room, cold air
Punched the doctor's face just like a cold fist;
Though he was expecting it to be warmer
Than the depressing and narrow hallway.

The agent opened one more door which let
Them into a smaller and colder room.

The Doctor is Asked to Degrade Himself

There was a stained bathtub, though nothing else:
No plumbing, no mats, no shower not even
A rusty hook to hang one's dirty clothes.

In the bathtub there was a frozen substance
Which could not be called water, for water
Was an insignificant part of it.

It had nauseating shades of colors.
The doctor did not want to assign a
Primary color to it, for it would have been
An insult to any proud and pure color.

He referred to it as the nauseating
Mixture of greenish bile and reddish blood.

When the agent informed him that this was
The substance in which he must take a bath,
The physician protested, "For God's sake,
Even a sewer rat won't lower itself
To crawl into this chunk of frozen sewage."

The agent firmly grabbed the doctor's arm
And ordered him to take off his clothing.

If it were one to one, the doctor was
In much better physical condition
Than that kid who were giving the orders.

Feeling like a Circus Tiger

The doctor felt like a circus tiger,
Which is not in its jungle but in a circus
Where a show man is cracking the whip.

In another ring, a tiger paws the air,
And intensifies the fire in its eyes
To dim the light of the ring of fire,
And obeys the ringmaster by jumping
Through the ring of fire and finishes the act.

In that horrid hell of a torture chamber
Which is called a shower, only fire was in
The eyes of the of the furious physician
Who was hoping to get through with that madness.

He took off his dirty clothes and used them
To slap the slimy face of that cold floor.

When he jumped into the tub, its wrinkled
Face of ice shattered like the shell of a
Rotten egg and released its foul odor,
And stirred up its contents of clotted blood,
Frozen pieces of stool and strands of hair.

He Was Forced to Smear Himself

He was forced to smear himself with that feces.
His cold hands moved on his body as if
They were lifeless hands of somebody else's.

Then the agent told the physician that
He must dunk his head under that foul hell.

The Doctor wanted to jump out and fight,
Though the agent had all the advantages.
The physician could not act fast enough
To free himself from that slippery slime.

The agent overpowered his victim,
And pushed his face under that putrid pit.

And kept Arpad's head under for a while,
For the doctor it felt like an eternity.

After releasing his head, the agent
Said, "I am sure you know what has happened.
You held your breath to prevent aspiration
Of that septic substance into your lungs,

And I did not keep your head under long
Enough to compel you to aspirate,
And develop an anaerobic lung abscess.

Who was that Agent?

The doctor reassessed the agent's psyche,
Who was he? A sadistic psychopath?
Or an agent of a foreign country?

Arpad would have been happy if that agent
Were an exception for the common folks.
If that was the case, he could forgive him.

The Agent's Critical Examination

Revealed that he was a normal young man,
But was brainwashed to believe in new doctrines.
He was not a villain but a victim.

The Doctor Wanted to Forgive

The doctor wanted to forgive the agent.
But he needed to discuss the issue
With someone with the same value system.
Though the folks were scared to open their mouths.

To his surprise the doctor himself found
That his own mandibular jaw was locked,
With anger and it could not be opened,
With a powerful pair of dental pliers.
He had no control over his emotions.

His mind was like a whirlpool, where his feelings
Would churn and then get sucked under without
A decisive victory or defeat.

In his mind discordant ideas would
Overlap so he would both seek vengeance,
And also forgiveness at the same moment.

Neither Arpad nor Eva ever disclosed
The identity of the tortured doctor.

We guessed who he was yet we did not ask,
Knowing that it could not change anything.

In the era of Communist Hungary
If you did not like what was going on,
The only option was to escape from the country.
Where you might end up was not a concern,
Only the getting out was important.

To escape from the country was risky.
One could be caught and taken to work camp.

It was a project that both of them could
Lose before reaching their destinations.

A traveling couple would draw attention.
So they decided to escape alone.

Since they were faced with numerous unknowns;
They could not make a plan and stick-to-it.

Childhood Memories of Arpad were Surfacing

To get away from the dilemmas of
The present, Arpad's mind went back to his childhood.

A bunch of boys were gathering dry straw,
And one of the boys was staying behind,
And preparing a smooth and sandy ground,
For he was the safe keeper of the jar.

The kids returned with their dry sheaves and
They sat down and wove a loose ring of straws.
Which was about four feet in diameter.

They fitted the straw ring around the dressed ground,
With their matches, they built a ring of fire.

The keeper of the jar dropped a scorpion
At the center of the fast burning ring of fire.

The scorpion ran wildly to find an exit.
When it could not find a passage to freedom,
It stopped at the middle of the ring of fire.
Then bent back its segmented tail and stung
Itself to inject a high dose of poison.

Arpad said, "When there is no road to freedom,
Then the suicide is an alternative."

Some other day the boys were together,
And one of them was carrying a jar.
And in that jar there were lazy beetles,
Though their bodies were heavily armored.

The keeper of the jar borrowed a beetle
And dropped it into his jar with a scorpion.
The boys were surprised to see that a sluggish
Beetle was devouring a poisonous creature.

Arpad said," Fast and furious can't win
All bouts that he happened to be engaged in.
Even slow and sluggish has its weapons.

One more about the boys: This time they were
Hiking at the foothills where a boy noticed
A small lizard which was sunning itself.
He grabbed its tail, and the lizard shed it,
And ran into a hole between the rocks.

Arpad said, "For living things to survive
They'd get rid of their accessory organs."

Making Plans to Escape from the Hungary

They fixed their gaze into the future;
What they have seen there was discouraging.

They listened to the sound of the future,
And what they have heard there was deafening.

False Promises of the Communists

Communists were promising a greener
Pasture to graze, provided that the folks
Could learn to live their lives like docile sheep.

Konyas Wanted to Control their Own Destiny

They decided to control their own destiny.
To do that, their only option was to
Get out of the country and be left out,
Reject all, and be rejected by all;
Leave behind what they loved and what they hated,
And what was evil and what was holy.

Once they decided to escape, their brains
Cooled down, and they became calculating.
They had a sense like a cold blooded lizard
Who could shed its tail in order to save its life.

To accomplish their goals, each one had to
Struggle alone and take big risks alone.

Each one of them could feel the suffering
Of the other but they could do nothing.

Only if they succeeded, then they could
Help each other with the healing process.

Refugee Camp at the Austria

With cool and calculating minds they planned.
They wanted to reach a refugee camp
Which was located in the eastern Austria.

Arpad was to do the initial try.
If he were successful, then Ewa were
To cross the border at its weakest point,
And ask to be assigned to the same camp.
Where her husband happen to be staying.

They sold everything they owned to raise enough
Currency to pay the people smugglers.
Though, they had not much to spare for themselves.
They divided the people smugglers' money.

They covered their diplomas with plastic,
And sewed them in the lining of their vests,
Which were never to be taken out until
They reached a refugee camp with some safety.

Calm surface waters were already tested.
Now it was the time to test the undercurrents.
Regardless, it was time to take some chances.

The Night Before the Separation

The night prior to Arpad's risky journey,
They forced together their entire lifetimes
Into a few hours just like a mayfly.

During a single night, they loved each other
Sufficient enough for a normal life time.

They tasted the disgusting taste of hate,
And at once they washed it out of their systems.

At the same time, they were both extremely close,
And also so far away from each other.

They saw the thin line in between despair,
And the hope and they held tight on to hope.

Togetherness and loneliness were twined
To create a unique sensation.
They felt the strength and the vulnerability,
Tenderness and the toughness in each other.

They valued the whisper of the spoken
Or the unspoken words of each other.
For they may never hear from each other again.

Arpad Crossed the Border

Sometime after their separation, Arpad
Crossed the border and reached to a refugee
Camp in Austria, which was an old castle.

We had no details about Arpad's escape.
We were never told as to how many
Attempts he made, and how long it took him
To arrive in Austria, or what kind
Of hardships he may have suffered during
The ordeal, and we never questioned him.

Eva's Botched-up Escape Plan

By the time Eva could establish her
Connections with the people smugglers,
Those networks were becoming riskier.

Even traveling inside the country
Was becoming restricted and controlled.

The government was issuing a passport
For every citizen which were to be
Used for traveling inside the country.

One were to carry his/her passport at
All times and to present it to the police
Or to the gendarme upon their request.

It was a very well known secret that
The internal passport was imposed upon
People so that the government could spy on
Its citizens as to where they are going.
And what they are intending to do?

International passports were a rare
Privilege for the trusted officials.

Eva Activated Her Escape Plan

Not to raise any suspicion, Eva
Were to take a short trip to Keszthely
Where her family owned a summer home,
And hang out there for a couple of weeks,
Then to shift further west to Szombathely.
As if she was to spend some time with an aunt.
For the sleuths it may look legitimate;
Though it was easy to see that she was
Moving closer to the Austrian border.

At Szombathely, she bought a bus ticket
To Budapest which were to pass through Gyor.
Thinking this route would give the impression
That she were going back to where she started.

Finding the Safe House

At Gyor she suddenly disappeared
Without claiming any of her luggage.

By following the signs, which were engraved
Deep into her brain, she found the safe house.
A motherly lady answered the bell.
In a hurry, they exchanged the code numbers.
Then Eva was allowed to go inside.

When Eva's heart stopped pounding in her chest,
And her hyperventilation was over,
She handed the money to the hostess
For the services to be rendered soon.

Instructions of the Mediator

The lady seized Eva's ID's and other
Papers that might direct the attention
Of the agents to their operation,
So that the agents would shut down their project,
Then who will help to the freedom seekers?

The intermediary lady gently
But firmly said, "From now on we will think that
We never met, and we don't know each other."

'In case any of you get caught, that should
Be all they could get into their hands:
No money, no names, no maps, and no comrades,
No simple clues to dig into it.

For your own protection you should memorize
Some false numbers to lead them to nowhere.
So they get frustrated and turn you loose."

The Eyes of Eva

The host looked deep into Eva's eyes
And said, "You're lucky being so puny,
That way you do not attract unwanted
Attention on the trails that may be watched.
Once you tuck your long hair under your cap,
They will take you for a thin teenage boy."

You'll proceed westward on a zigzag path.
Make sure that the river is to the north,
And you are always facing to the west.

Consider the rivers as the umbilical
Cords that is connected to the freedom.

First follow the south loop of the Danube.
When you reach the Masonmagyarovar,
Without failing follow the Leitha River.

Each day you will be instructed regarding
Your progress and your next day rendezvous.
If you can't reach your destination,
Do not panic, and do not take chances.
When it's safe, we'll look for you the next day.

When you are ten miles east of the border,
Our help will end, and you'll be on your own.

At the border crossing to the Austria,
Some prefer the land and some swim the river.

When you reach the border strip, be careful
For there is a small Russian presence there.

When the Leitha River meanders towards
The southwest, cross it there to its west shore
If you can reach that shore, you'll be safe,
But not necessarily welcome for these
Days are rough times for the Austrians as well.

Eva had warm feelings towards the lady,
And the organization that she is
Belonged to; for the service that they provide
Is not given just for the money they receive.

Metamorphoses of Eva

While Eva was searching for freedom,
She metamorphosed and felt like she were
Two persons wrapped together in one skin.

Her beliefs were not as positive as
They had been before, and her doubts were not
As negative, as they had been before.

She could not discern, distinctly established
Boundaries, between the right and the wrong.
She saw no traitors and no heroines.

She realized, that for the first time in
Her life, the gain is not a payment for
The loss, nor the profit is a reward.
They merely coexist like the peaks and
The valleys of any well lived life.

With each step taken, was she nearing to
Her destination or was she cutting
Her ties from everything she loved for so long?

Was she deserting her sick motherland?
Or was she reaching to a normal life?
Or was she lost in a desert of doubts?

She noticed physical changes as well.
Her night vision grew so keen that she was
Able to see things better than a night owl.
She convinced herself that nothing is mute.

When she listened to the ground, it would tell her that
An out-of -sight horse is running or galloping;
And what direction it is heading?

The little birds are the best companions,
For anyone who's alone and afraid.
By their presence, even when they are silent,
They assure one that she is not alone.

Even a nervous body can relax,
When those song sparrows are cheerfully chirping.
And one can feel safer when they are singing.
One must be cautious when they're alarmed.

Eva's sense of smell grew so acute that without
The help of other senses she could
Smell the river and adjust her directions.

She learned how the life-giving sun could squeeze
The life out of a woman's healthy skin.

How a soft breeze can sandpapers her skin raw,
And how the salt of one's sweat keeps them open,

How the cheekbones come out and flaunt themselves,
How the walking can burn the body fat.

When the body melts away, how the eyes
Grow larger to reflect the light of life.

The Day of Deliverance and Eva's Apprehension

After all those days of preparation
And planning, there came the day of deliverance.

She carefully chose her crossing point,
Though, she could not feel the undercurrent
Before jumping into the river itself.

While she was struggling to save her life,
Strong undercurrents carried her into
The waiting arms of the Russian soldiers.
She was taken to the army barracks.

The next day, Russian soldiers were herding
That mixed flock towards a rundown rail road station,
Ten miles away from the holding barracks.

From the barracks they were to be shipped to their
Home Town, there they will be judged and punished.

Inmates of the barracks were all guilty
Of the same crime: Not being a tame sheep,
And straying away from the official flock.

There were about three dozen of worn out,
Broken-down and defeated Hungarians:
Females, Males, Children, Youth and Elderly.
Yet a silent bond was connecting them.

When Eva started her escape project,
She was weighing merely ninety-nine pounds,
Which fell down to a skeletal eighty-eight pounds.

She was no longer scared of anything;
What could have gone wrong already went wrong.
She was day dreaming and falling behind.

Suddenly she felt an excruciating
Pain in the middle of her shoulder blades,
When she turned her dreamy eye back to see
What it was, her eyes met with the cold blue eye
Of a Russians soldier on horse back.
He said, "You thieving and tricky Gypsy,
You better not dare to play games with me

If there were a running competition
With a prize, I'd bet on you to win it.

You must hurry to catch up with the rest,
Unless you'd like to be skinned with this horse whip."

Humiliation coupled with anger,
Pumped fresh adrenaline into her system,
And in no time she caught up with the rest.

Yet she was unable to calm herself down.
She wanted to whip someone with her tongue.

She mumbled about the Russian soldier, "Dumb Muzhik.
In a beauty queen you can't see the beauty.

There are people in this world with good taste;
They will recognize me for what I am.

"Your image of a beautiful lady
Is a long potato for a body,
And a couple of toothpicks for the legs."

Eva Was Taken Back to Budapest

And kept in jail to brake her willpower.
When the agents thought that she were soft enough
For the interrogation, they began to play their cat-and-
mouse game.

The initial phase consisted of neglect.
The officials were patiently waiting,
For her willpower to completely vanish.

When the time was just right for the agents,
They began questioning. "You are a smart lady.
You understand we won't wait till fall,
So that we can pick up the leaves as they fall.
We must get down to the roots of this crime.
We must have the names of your accomplices."

Eva's Answers

Eva, "Sorry. They must have given me
The false names that will not lead to real people."
Over and over, "We must have the names."
Eva, "All I have are false code names."

Agent, "Where is your husband?"
Eva, "I don't have a husband;
We'd been separated for some time.
The war tears all things apart but mends none."

Eva was physically too frail to torture.
Yet, she was too strong-minded to break down.
So they threw her out in the unsafe streets,
Just like an unwanted helpless kitten.

She treaded towards the shores of the Danube,
To reconnect with the city's land marks.

She found herself at the top of a bluff,
Looking down at the churning white waters
Which could drown anybody's suffering.
She heard herself saying, "How can you do
This to Arpad? He is waiting for you."

Then a love song of her teenage years started.
Then she noticed the distant blinking lights
Of the open-air teahouses which had been
There since the Ottoman centuries.

Her family used to take her to one
Of those teahouses where they played love songs.
One of those songs echoed in Eva's mind.

"My eyes are searching all over for you,
To cherish and to adore you.
This world flaunts its girls as it turns,
Yet never can I ignore you"

Going to Her Mother-in-Law's House

When she reached her mother-in-law's house,
Mrs. Konya was locking the front door.
She was all dressed up with her Sunday best.
She did not want to be late to the Church.

Mrs. Konya looked into the big eyes
Of that girl and thought that there was something
Familiar about that mysterious girl,
Although, she could not be sure who she was.
To make it to the church in time, Mrs. Konya
Decided to cut to the chase, and then direct
Questions started to roll out of her mouth:

"How may I help you? For whom are you looking?
Who are you?" Eva responded, "Mother,
I do not know who I am anymore!

Am I an empty shell without a core?
Or am I a body without a soul?"
I came here with a dim hope that you might
Know what could be the answer to this puzzle."

Mrs. Konya Recognizes Her Daughter-in-Law

After hugging each other, they went limp.
Sometime later, by supporting each other,
They went inside and dropped upon a sofa.
For a while they let the cascading tears wash
Their faces which also soothed their souls.

Before long they were reminiscing of
The happy days they had not too long ago.

The fear and dismay were disappearing.
The vacuum that was left behind was
Filling with certainty of a brighter future,
And they were daring to dream of brighter days.

Every Stage of New Life Affects Everyone

Mrs. Konya said, "Every stage of life
Has its blessings and its impediments;
When the destiny deals you a bum hand
In your old age, you don't have much to lose
For you have already used up your days.

"When the inflation wipes out savings
Of the elderly, they'll have no time
To recuperate and not much time to suffer.

"New governments, new policies may come,
And they may go, yet one thing will not change,
"All governments will neglect the elderly.
And hope that they'll soon fill a hole in the ground;
Thus the government won't have to take care of them.

"Youth is liquid. They can run around
In the springs and can evaporate during the summers.
They can't be locked before they reach to their goal.

"We can't expect to hear directly from Arpad,
But mother's intuition tells me that
He found a hole in that iron curtain,
To pass through and embrace the freedom.
Eva, there's a hole for you to pass through".

Emil said to Isabella, "Don't
Probe old wounds. We've never asked how many
Trials it took for Eva to cross the border."
She did not talk pertaining to that painful
Phase of her life and we asked no questions.

The Refugee Camp in Austria

Prior to Eva's arrival, Arpad
Had a full time job? in Austria.

Every day he'd get up and without shaving
Or taking a shower, he would rush to
The refugee center to check the list
Of new comers and then crosscheck it again,
Giving consideration for the possible
Misspelling of Hungarian names,
Plus possible use of the maiden names.
Once again he would look for the birthdays
Column and crosscheck the name.

Eva Arrives at the Refugee Camp

One day he found the name with the correct spelling,
And the birthday matched, and she was from Hungary.

Without saying anything, he stepped outside
To get his face slapped by the cold air,
To be sure that he was not daydreaming.
He ran back into the office to fill
Out the necessary papers for the
Reunification of the couples.

Reunification of Eva and Arpad

Suddenly shelter, food, and fuel
Became very important for Arpad.

Since he had a family, he was assigned
To a cell in an abandoned castle.

When Eva and Arpad were reunited
They fused to form a perfect whole again,

Through their windowless cell they'd see the world,
Even though the walls, floor, and ceiling
Were cold since the fireplace had not been lit by
Anybody since the time of the Serfs.
The only heat they could rely on was
The heat that their bodies could generate.
The temperature of their room was not even like a cave's
For it was not the same during the summer and the winter.

Trying to Find a Country
Where to Live Permanently

They spent their days filling out applications
To many countries that might accept them,
Preferably, as permanent residents.

They also spent time by scavenging,
In the ash pile, for reusable cinders.

The meals were always tasteless and meager.
If one of them wanted to treat the other,
All she/he could offer was the last morsel
On their plate, saying "Please finish what is
Left on my plate; I can't take one more bite."

A Frozen Potato

One of those cold midnights they were starving,
The only food they had was a frozen potato,
But they had no source of heat to cook it.

Limited License to Practice Medicine

The lights of the future began to flicker.
Arpad was granted a limited license
To practice medicine in the hard to
Reach and isolated alpine villages.

Every morning he would get on his skis,
Hit the trail, and in the evening he'd return,
Not with cash, but with food and fuel:
Home cured meat, eggs, butter and coal to cook.

They had regained the weight that they had lost.
Eva's complexion was glowing, and her
Abdomen was getting rounder and bigger.
They had enough food for three to thrive.

Birth of a Baby Boy

When their baby boy was born, they started
To see their world with different eyes.
They called their cell as the suite of the prince,
The castle became the principality.

In their dreams they got rid of the borders,
And for their son, they wished a peaceful world.
Their son died before he could walk or talk.
We were not told, what was the cause of death,
And we never had the courage to ask.

Once more they stopped dreaming and looked into
The reality from another angle.
They saw stonewalls, stone ceiling, stone floor,
And referred to their cell as "The Grave".
They retailored their dreams enough for two.

Reentering the World
Through Pakistan

Arpad received an acceptance contract
From Pakistan to work as a surgeon,
In one of the best surgical hospital.

He signed the contract immediately,
Because that contract meant many things for them.
They were going to get out of that stone grave.

They were no longer going to feel
As if they were no more than parasites.
They were going to have legal status
To say, "I'm sorry, I can't do that for
What you are asking me to do isn't in my contract."

At that time, Pakistan was a new country
With millions of refugees of their own.
Resources were few, needs were plenty.
Colonial power still held great influence.

Walking on Similar Paths

Eva and Arpad felt comfortable
To work with and to live with nice people
Who lived, walked and worked on parallel paths.

The Surgery of Khalil Khan

Mr. Khan required a risky surgery.
Since he was an old man with other ailments,
The risk of the surgery was quite high.

Arpad thought he could pull him through the surgery.
Yet even more skillful Pakistani
Surgeons did not dare to touch to that gentleman.

They had a case review conference to
Reach a decision as to what approach
Was a suitable one for this man,
Both medically and politically,
They voted to send him to London.
Arpad insisted that the surgery
Could be performed in Pakistan with an even
Lower mortality rate than in London.

The Pakistani surgeons stated that
The problem was the Mr. Khan's tribesmen.
They may not accept any complications.

Arpad may regard Mr. Khan as a
Harmless, saintly old man, but we know better.
He's the revered and powerful patriarch
Of the rebellious Afridi Tribe.

Dr. Yahya, Chief of Surgical Service
Said," We all can do the procedure with
Accepted setbacks and mortality.

In this case, if the result is less
Than expected, his tribesman may not wait,
For a fact finding medical review.

If they think that less than the best care was given,
They won't sue the hospital or the surgeon,
But right then and there, they pass judgment
As to what kind of action should be taken.

If the Afridies were to seek revenge,
They metamorphose into vile Afrets.

They stir at the Spin Ghar Range and gather
Strength at the Khyber Hills. Then fall upon
Us like the locust to devour everything,
Including the hospital, stone by stone.

Arpad visited Mr. Khan and told
Him that unless he signs the informed consent
Form which states, "I willingly choose to have
My surgery under Dr. Konya's
Care and I refuse to go to London,"
Otherwise I cannot work on your case.

Mr. Khan said, "Young man, you have a way
To make simple things complex. I will sign no
Paper, for a piece of paper provides
No more protection than a paper shield,
But a man's spoken word is everything."

"There was a time when naught existed but God.
When He said one word, 'Exist.' then suddenly
The whole universes came into existence.
When he chooses to say, "Cease," everything
Shall go back to God, and all shall be one."
A word is the Beginning and the Ending.

He turned to his clansman and slowly said,
"I have no claim of any kind on this
Soul here and now, and no claim here and after."

He asked Arpad to repeat the same words.
Arpad said the same words; then they shook hands.

Mr. Khan continued, "We live and die
For our spoken words, since those words shall stay
Forever in the book of eternity."

The operation was successful, and
The post surgical care was meticulous.
Possible complications were predicted,
And preventative measures were taken.

When Mr. Khan was fit to be discharged,
He said to Arpad, "You and I are now
Friends without indebtedness to each other.

I did plan to steal a couple of days
From the "Time" which is the eternal robber of lives.
I hope you'll be my partner in that crime.

You will receive my invitation when
The snow recedes and the blue and yellow
Crocuses sprout at the rims of the snow patches,
The time at which the Kayber Hills are at their best."

Konyas Grew Contented with Their Lives

In general, Konyas began to be
Contented with their lives in Pakistan.
At this phase of their lives, they had the means
And the time to pursue other interests.

Eva considered photography
Much more than a hobby. To her it was an art form.
They proudly supported the fine arts.

They commissioned a famous and busy
Painter to do a portrait of Eva.

In the eyes of his mind, the painter must have
Seen her as a queen, for he got her to
Pose like a recently crowned young queen,
Elizabeth II. Even today, one
Can see the regal demeanor on that
Portrait, with or without the regal crown.
What's more, she didn't grow older with the aging
Process, like the regal queen had done.

When the winter snow was actually melting
On he Kayber highland and the crocuses
Were blooming, Afridi clansmen came
To escort the Konyas to the Kayber

Highlands where they were to have a celebration
Mostly to honor Konyas as one of their clan.

For a while they drove traveled on a fairly
Well maintained roads which soon started to gain
Altitude with a constant twisting upward.

They came to a point where the spring rains had
Washed out the road, making it impossible
For the pick-ups to work. So they parked them.

A group of young men were waiting with their
Horses to give rides for the invitees.

These riding horses were well trained and sturdy.
They were well acclimated to the thin air.

When the traveling party arrived at
A less steep terrain, stone houses exposed
Themselves on the sides of the high cliffs.

The villages were built on a larger
Mesa which was surrounded with deep canyons,
And a narrow neck that connected the
Mesas with the high mountains all around.

The villages were locate where they
Can be easily defendable.

This has allowed the Afridis to maintain
Their ways of lives, and identities for
Thousands of years without outside interference.

They stopped in front of a stately building.
When they dismounted, they discovered that
The nostrils of the horses were flaring red
For they were circulating their blood faster
So that they could extract extra oxygen.

Mr. Khan greeted them in front of the
Guest house which was next to the headquarters.
After exchanging good will and pleasantries,
Konyas retired and had a restful night.

The next late afternoon everything was
Ready for a major celebration
At the headquarters building: The music,
The dancing, the food, the sweets, and everything.

The only thing left to do was to enjoy.
And the folks had a memorable time.

Mr. Khan said, "Last night we had a meeting
Of the elders and decided to grant
Afridi citizenship to the Konyas".
When he asked if there were any objections,
The folk said, "We honor our new citizens."

A Dagger as a Seal of Acceptance

When the folks wound down, Mr. Kahn opened
A safety deposit box and took out
An object, which was wrapped in green velvet.
He unwrapped it and took out a dagger.
Its handle was ivory, carved and also
Encrusted with Turquoise and other gemstones.

"This dagger is a key to open every
Afridi door; from now on you and your
Clan is full citizens of the Afridis."

Konyas spent their special night peacefully,
However, Arpad was so excited
That his eyelids were dancing all night long.

Arpad understood what a tribal dagger,
With symbolic notches on its hilt meant.

It was not a metal passport without
An expiration date, or a contract,
But an object which was symbolizing
A total acceptance by a free tribe.
On Arpad'spart, it was a reentry into
A close knit society as an equal.

Since ancient times, Afridi people had
Been the gatekeepers of the Kyber Pass.

Herodotus wrote about their control
Over the high passes, and the people
Either fought their way through,
Or they sought their neutrality
On their way in or way out from India.

The following men passed through the Kyber Pass.
Darius I the Great, Alexander
The Great, Mahmud of Ghazna, Tamerlane
And the British Empire with their vast resources.

The geographical makeup of the pass
Is such that it favors the Afridis.

On a high and long pass, they could choose where
To fight and where to let them advance to
The next trap, where they would have the advantage.

They could rain arrows on the passing armies
Without being seen. When pushed hard, they would
Pull back to the Spin Ghar Range's safety.

No tough man or stout horse could climb those mountains;
Unless they were born and raised on those highlands.
Afridis let you pass when they wanted to.

Konyas are Moving to the U.S.A.

When Arpad's contractual obligations
Were pleasantly finished in Pakistan,
They moved to the USA with the hope
That they could settle there permanently.

Once more he had to start from the beginning.
Once more he'd be a novice in a new land.
Once more he'd be pushing the same stone uphill.

By law he had to finish an internship,
In an accredited teaching hospital,
To be able to obtain a license
To practice medicine in the USA.
In addition to that, he had to have three years
Of surgical Residency, to be qualified as a surgeon.

He finished his internship and surgical
Residency, at Johns Hopkins Hospital.

He passed the state board and the National
Surgical Specialty Board examinations.

New Developments

Once more he felt like he was reborn.
He packed his diplomas and moved to Spokane.
There, he established a successful practice.

For Arpad, working hard was not a hardship.
When things looked tough, he re-examined
His own past, which lightened his present burden.
Since he never had shortcuts in his life,
He never sought shortcuts in his practice.

There were no poor or rich; all had one life.
Every time he'd cut, everyone would bleed.
If it were not controlled, they'd exsanguinate.

The Beginning of Poor Health

On one typical morning he found out that
His legs could no longer support his weight.
His neurologist diagnosed it as
A rare case of Guillain-Barre Syndrome.
He had no legs to stand up to fight, or
To find a neutral ground, to reorganize.

He Sold His Practice

For the first time in his life, he started
To make big decisions while lying down.

He took a retirement and sold his practice.
He tried to keep his mind and hands busy.
Yet the pain in his legs grew intolerable.

Eva was Taking Over
More Obligations

At the same time, he was thankful and resentful.
He tried to solve his problem permanently.
He took his gun in his hand and pointed
It to his skull but could not pull the trigger
For he remembered a patient of his
Who pulled the trigger, however he survived
The damages done by the passing bullet,
Save, he lead a vegetative existence.

He put his gun down to think and find
A better way to end his misery.

He took his stethoscope and listened to
His heart sounds and palpated, his left side
Of his chest to find the exact location
Of the apex of his heart and then aimed
As such that the bullets could pass through the apex
Of his heart and pierce through his aorta.

He did not have the strength to pull the trigger,
For he had a young patient who attempted
To take his life and pulled the trigger.
The bullet missed his heart but logged in
His spinal canal of that young man who
Survived but lived as a paraplegic.

The possibility of survival
With an infirmity was not an option.

So, he wanted to end it all without
Any possibility of survival.

He thought that the best way to end it all,
Sans survival was exsanguination.
The life would be drained out of the body;
No visible gore would be left behind.

He planned to cut his femoral artery.
The spurted blood could be cleaned easily
From the porcelain bathtub and the tiles
On the wall, and the plastic shower curtains.

The mortician could use the already
Prepared vessel for the embalming fluids.

An Inner Voice Sobered Him

When he was ready to cut the artery,
His inner voice asked, "How can you do this
To Eva?" He answered back, "No, I can't
Leave her all alone." He accepted his fate.

After long-term physical therapy,
Use of prosthetics and exercises,
In time he became ambulatory,
Which gave him his self pride and independence.

Isabella Asked

Isabella asked, "Didn't these folks know
Something about the American dream?
Or did they not wish to take part in it?"

Emil replied, "They surely participated
In the American Dream: A stately
House in the suburbs with a swimming pool,
A manicured yard and tamed shrubs with flowers.

Also a beach house on Lake Pend Oreille.
Yet for them, dreaming the common dream was
Not by itself completely satisfying.

Konyas' Private Dreams

The two of them dreamed their private dreams as well.
They've never said whether owning a piece
Of pine forest with a blockhouse on it
Was a part of their private dreams or not.
We have never asked, though we have felt that
While they were refugees in Austria,
They were starving but all they had was
A frozen potato but no fuel to cock it.

They must have promised to themselves, "We'll find
A country on this planet where we don't
Have to live in someone else's cold castle.
Instead we will posses our own warm house
On acres of land. There, we will raise our
Own potatoes and cut our own firewood to bake it.
We will never end up with a frozen
Potato and no heat source to bake it."
That is why their cellar is always filled year-round
With potatoes that they can't consume.

Their firewood is stacked like library
Books, dusty but dry, ready to be lit.

Are the Konyas Escaping From the Society?

Isabella, "Isn't that, in a way,
Escaping from the society and
Letting the mainstream of life pass you by?"

Emil, "No, it's more like flying higher
Into the life in order to palpate
The ever pulsating life energy,
And feel like one is near to life itself."

The Konyas Develop New Interests

After the initial shock of retirement,
They saw it as an opportunity
To do the things that they liked to do anyhow.

Eva developed a keen awareness
Of beauty beneath the shell of all things,
And caught that beauty with her camera.

Arpad already knew about the common
Problems of Native Americans.
Still he was appalled that not a single
Significant remnant of the Pend Oreilles
Were present, on the lands of their ancestors.

Wars Can't Annihilate Nations

The nations of the world warred with each other,
And left behind genocides and mass graves.
Even then, some people of the defeated
Nations survived to tell the war stories,
Provided that the defeated nations
Had their daily bread to hang on and prosper.

The Pend Oreilles

The Pend Oreilles did not perish because
Of donated blankets with smallpox viruses,
Or other diseases brought by white men.

They moved for not having good economy.
The Pend Oreille people were hunters and gatherers.
Because of that, they had to have large areas of land
To dig for roots and to collect berries.
They had to have animals to hunt for meat,
And fish to catch and to process for the winter.

When there were no buffalo herds to hunt,
And not enough territory to gather,
They had to move on and leave their lands behind.

Wars of Ages

Since the beginning, mankind developed
Big plans, to make war on their own species.

Nations viciously fought with each other
All through history without any respite.

The thought of war is brought to action by
A gene which nests on the Y-chromosome.

The mother of wars was the Trojan Wars;
For romance was involved, and gods took sides.
It lasted long enough which was ten years.
The victory was taken with trickery,
And the entire nation was massacred.

Since then there has been wars for all reasons;
The Crusaders to gain power and revenge,
The Civil War, World War I, World War II.

The best way to prevent future wars
May be:" To forgive and to forget."
Yet at this time, we are not ready to
Follow this policy. On the contrary,
All we hear is, "Don't forget World War I,
World War II, Vietnam, Korean and many other wars."

I say, "Forget the World War I. Forget
The World War II. Forget the Pearl Harbor.
Forget everything that had to do with war,
And don't forget to forget the Alamo.

Don't waste energy tearing down the war
Reminders; let the time do its magic,
So that the cobwebs can decorate them.

Selma Seeker

Arpad heard that there is a Pend Oreille
Storyteller by the name of Selma Seeker,
Who lives with the Kalispell Indians.
He wished to hear the story of the Pend Oreilles
From the mouth of a member of those people.

When Arpad and Eva had their first visit
With Selma, they were certain that she was
A genuine storyteller with confidence.

"She was willing to talk but careful not
To reveal the real story without control.

She wanted to know if they owned a boat,
And, if so, would they be willing
To ferry her to Memaloose Island
On the certain spiritual occasions.

She also enjoyed visiting the other
Smaller islands of the Lake Pend Oreille.

Selma gave her age as, "I have been living
Since I was born." The wrinkles on her face
Were making such an unusual pattern
That no one could guess her age or her race.

She had been telling her stories so long
That they grew to be a part of herself.
As she rocked to the rhythm of her chanting,
Her hair would ripple as if it is starting
From the past and extending to the future.

Her audience would have a feeling that
She might have personally witnessed
The events that might have taken place.

During their visits, mostly Selma talked,
And they listened without questioning.
For them just the story was important.
Whether it was true or not, did not matter.

It became a habit for them to take
The long loop from Spokane to the Kalispell
Reservation, pick up Selma and
Drive to the lake, and then sail for her
Pilgrimage at the Memaloose Island.

When they would land at the shores of the island,
Selma would ask Konyas to wait in the boat.
And not to go deep into the island.
She would chant a short passage and then wait
For a short while as if expecting instructions
From the spirits as to what to do next?

And then she would slowly advance into
The forest and disappear for a while.

When she would return, she'd act like a person,
Who had had a spiritual experience.
Then, for her, the day's work would be finished,
And she'd ask to be driven back to her home.

Sometime later, she told Arpad that she
Had obtained permission from the spirits.
From now on, he may accompany her on
Her special pilgrimages of the islands.

She would lead, and he'd follow her footsteps.
When she felt like it, she'd chant in Pend Oreille,
And then translate it into English.

The Elder Ones

Human nature being what it is?
Elders got tired of following the straight path.
So even the elders were infested
With the plague of megalomania,
Which sealed tight their hearts and ears, so that they
Could not hear voices of the common sense.

All they could hear was the echoes of their
Own meaningless words in their hollow skulls.
They persuaded themselves that they were not
A part of the whole but the whole itself.

What was even worse, grandfathers grew greedy,
And they forgot the needs of their grandsons.
They started to take from Mother Earth more
Then she could give without being depleted.

The Great Spirit warned them, through medicine men,
About the consequences of their greed,
But they would not listen to the warnings.

They continued to attend sacred dances,
Not to worship but to use those occasions
To arouse their sensual sentiment.

The Great Spirit no longer could tolerate
All that filth on the face of Mother Earth.
He decided to cleanse the entire Earth.

The Great Spirit Cleans the Earth.

One night he sent the spirit of the winds.
He took a deep breath and inhaled all good
People and good creatures into his lungs.
He then slowly turned towards the Happy
Hunting Grounds and exhaled those chosen ones.

As it was meant to be, all living things
Started to live in peace and harmony.

The next, he sent the spirit of water.
He caused a great flood to scrub the Earth lean.
When the land regained its vitality,
Lake Pend Oreille became Life's Blue Eyes.
The Spirit of Wind went back to the happy
Hunting grounds and inhaled the living things,
Then he turned around and exhale
Them all around the shores of Lake Pend Oreille.

Two Medicine Men

To maintain the peace among the living,
They were guided by two medicine men.
One of them resided on the mainland,
And the other one at Memaloose Island.

Mainland medicine man tutored the young
And kept them in line and consoled the old.

When someone died or broke the laws of the tribe,
That person was sent to Memaloose Island,
Which was a burial ground for the dead,
And a sanctuary for the living.

Island medicine man buried the dead,
And purified the souls of the sinners.

When a soul broke the taboos of his tribe,
And was sent to the island, the medicine man
Would cleanse his soul and send that person back
To his family and tribe the same day.

If the person were to commit a crime,
Then it might take a long time for his soul
To become clean and fit to live with others.

In some cases the medicine man would give
A new name and a new identity
To the offenders and they had to start
From the beginning to build a new life.

For a long time, people lived according
To the master design for all creatures.
One felt the pains and pleasures of others.
They hunted and caught salmon, barely
Enough to meet their nutritional needs.

In spring pathfinders scattered in all directions
To find food and process it for the winter.

In late fall, they returned to the delta
Of the Clark Fork River for their dugout houses.

In time the people once more grew wicked.
During that time Spotted Coyote
Was the medicine man of the mainland,
And Wide Eyed Owl was the medicine man
Of Memaloose and the other islands.

Wide Eyed Owl dealt with the extreme ends of life,
And with the unwanted crises of life.

They brought newborn babies to him to name
And bless them to grow to be decent beings.

For burial, bodies would be transported
With dugout canoes to Memaloose Island,
And the bodies would be left on the burial
Boulder at the dock, for purification.

Families and friends would not be allowed
To step, much less to wander, on the island,
For it is belong to the resident spirits.

People are welcome to visit their loved ones,
Only on special ceremonial days.

Immediately Wide Eyed Owl and his
Apprentice, Little Fox, would start the cleansing
Process by washing the body with water
From the Lake Pend Oreille as they chanted hymns,
From the sacred sayings of the Pend Oreilles.

They anoint the entire body
With beaver oil and fill the mouth with dried
Syringa flowers to make it easy
For the soul to come out of the body,
And journey to the Great Spirit to unite.

They'd gently cross the arms over the chest,
Then they'd lay the right hand over the heart.
Then they'd hang the remains with rawhide ropes
From a tall pine and turned the face toward
The east to catch the first rays of the sun.

They would never bury under the soil
For fear that the soul might be imprisoned.

They'd paint the bodies with red and white paint
To stop stray ghosts from getting hold of the soul.
They'd put on the decedent's ceremonial
Clothing, to make the bodies attractive.

Once More Harmony Fell Apart

The harmony that existed between people
And cosmic forces slowly fell apart.
This disintegration showed its effect
In every aspect of tribal affairs.

Some of the people, who were purified
At Memaloose Island and reunited
With their folks, were adopting their old ways,
And were disturbing the peace of the people.
These problems were crippling the tribal council.

When there are many questions but no answers,
People start to point fingers at each other.
Yet the fingers didn't know the right direction.

Spotted Coyote claimed that Wide Eyed Owl
Lost his old purifying medicine.
He was no longer fit to cleans the souls.

This had a grave consequence for the people.
If souls were not pure enough to unite
With Great Spirit, they would linger around
The Pend Oreille land to disturb the living.

Wide Eyed Owl claimed that Spotted Coyote
Was not instructing people properly
About the importance of harmonization

Of their lives with nature all around them.
By the time they come under my care,
Their souls are already crusted with sin,
So that it is impossible to cleanse them.

For the folk, the concerns would be same.
Toward the end of the winter, storytellers'
Tales would grow stale. When the food supplies drop
Low people's patience wore thin with each other.

Pathfinders would take to the trails to survey
The land and mark the most suitable trails.
As they went, they'd set their traps. On their way
Back to their winter settlement, they would
Pick up whatever was caught on their traps.

When the pathfinders returned from different
Directions, each one of them would report
About what they had seen. The Chief and Council
Would choose as to when and where to go first.

Pathfinders were the pride of their nation.
They were selected and trained carefully.
Their bodies were stout, and their words were truthful.
A successful year depended upon
Their astute observations and statements.

A Friend of all Living Things

At that unusual year, pathfinders witnessed
Something they had never seen before.
They saw the tracks of the buffalo and elk.
Yet, fresh tracks did not lead them to a herd.
They checked their traps and snares; they held nothing.
Instead they saw the footprints of a child.
They followed the footprints to track and catch
That mischievous child, but foot prints
Led them to the dens of grizzlies or wolves.

Neither Chief Black Bear nor the members of
The Council could doubt the words of the pathfinders.
Still they had no explanation as to
How can a child outwit their pathfinders?

From where could he come? Who are his parents?
Regardless, the officials have to stop him,
For his acts are threatening the food supply.

Wild Child and Spotted Coyote

Their attempts to capture and tame him failed.
Then they asked Spotted Coyote to lure
Him to join the tribe with his medicine.
He said, "Have you forgotten the words which
Were uttered by Grandfathers long ago?"
Great Spirit told them, he will not cleanse this
Land with flood nevermore. He'll let people
Do it with the help of a Seer to come.

Helper Spirit

This child is that promised Helper Spirit.
At this time he is learning his first lesson.
Until he completes his learning, he won't
Join us for we have nothing to offer.

He seeks harmony between living things.
He has no enemies; he needs no allies.

You see him as a child without a home.
For a mother bear, he's another cub.
For a mother buffalo, he is a calf.

Ever since I have arrived to this world,
I have been attempting to penetrate
The animal world to complete my learning.
Thus far, I've not been able to do so.

As you can see, disharmony and schism
Reign on this land which will lead to destruction
Of both human and animal domains.
Unless we unite with this Helper Spirit,
And come into harmony with the cosmos.

I have a plan to lure him to join our tribe.
But it will work only when he completes
His schooling in the animal kingdom.

By the age of puberty, He'll graduate
From the School of the Animal Kingdom,
And He'll be interested in the men's wisdom.

Spotted Coyote monitored the growth
Of the boy and when he noticed that his muscles
Began to bulge, he came closer to people.

When the time was right, he sent his daughter,
White Daisy, to the distant shores of the Lake
Pend Oreille to camp alone and have fun.

Soon she returned with the youth at her side.
Spotted Coyote named the youth Chalax.

From the beginning, the old medicine man
And Chalax, the mysterious young man,
Developed a unique relationship.
Both souls were a master and an apprentice.
They were learning veiled secrets from each other.

The Passing of Spotted Coyote

When the learning and teaching were completed,
Spotted Coyote left this world behind,
To continue with the next stage of his journey.

Chief Black Bear, with the consent of the Tribal
Council, appointed Chalax as medicine man,
Though folks did not have enough information
To feel good about the new appointee.

Yes, it was said that he was a bridge in
Between the animal's and men's kingdoms.
But should he be welcome to their lodges?

Celebration of the Soul of Spotted Coyote

It was a tribal tradition to get
Together on the fortieth day of
A person's death and celebrate his soul.

This year it was going to be a special
One for it was for Spotted Coyote.

Cross-Questioning of Chalax

After the feasting, after the drumming,
After the dancing, all ages gathered
Around a circle and started to ask
Questions which were directed at Chalax.

Chief Black Bear said, "Your childhood development
Was different than any other child.
We like to hear an answer from your mouth:
From where do you come and where do you go?"

Origin of Chalax

Before the beginning of this universe
All things were just one, a whole without parts,
And that seamless whole was the Great Spirit.

He could have created this Universe,
Without any preexisting atom.
Instead, He took a piddling particle
From himself and called it the Universe.

I took the past and filled it into the
Skin of the present. Then called it Chalax.
Now I'm emptying it into the feature,
To complete the mysterious cycle.
Thus, I will reunify with the Great Spirit.

Yet I'll never wholly know the Great Spirit.
A grain of sand is a part of the Universe!
How much a grain of sand knows of theUniverse?

One person's idea of happiness
Can't be transferred to another person.
Yet one goes there with his hopes and expectations;
For each person remembers his pleasant times
And dwelling on those times gives happiness.

There are no idol times to cause boredom.
One will not have everything but one will
Be satisfied with what one might possess.

An old man asked about the Happy Hunting Grounds.
He said, "If we know that the Happy Hunting
Ground functions with the rule of "peace for all"
We will be happy to accept all living
Creatures as members of our family."

When we take a look at the broad picture
Of nature, we will realize that nothing
Is worthless, and nothing is overwhelming.

Live in harmony with living things and
Do not take anything from them unless
They can easily afford to donate.

A young mother, as she pressed her baby
To her breast, asked, "What's the fate of this baby,
And the fortune of those yet to be born?"

He said, "Newborns are a promise for the future.
You don't choose them; luckily you're chosen.
Each baby arrives without any sin;
Their parents' sins can't be inherited."

Acceptance of Chalax by the People

After the question and answer session
With Chalax, the people felt that he is a
Caring person. So they accepted him
As a member of their society,
As well as their spiritual guide.

While he functioned as a medicine man,
He healed the sick, consoled the dejected,
Wed the lovers, and blessed the new born babies,
And closed the eyelids of the deceased souls.

Prophecies of Chalax Regarding the War Activities with Blackfeet

People were much interested with war
Activities of the Blackfeet. They wanted
Him to prophesy as to when they will
Attack and how big their forces shall be?

Chalax went through the routine rituals:
The meditation, the cleansing steam baths.
Then, each time he accurately predicted
When they will attack and how strong they'll be.

During the intertribal competitions,
The champion of the Blackfeet, Gray Wolf, used to
Win the games and walk away with the prizes.

When Chalax started to train the Pend Oreille
Youth, it became hard for Gray Wolf to win.
So they wanted to assassinate Chalax.
It did not work, for Chalax could change shape.
He may be singing on a lofty tree
Without being recognized by the Blackfeet.

When he grew older, he began to see
Life from a different perspective.

The future life of the society
Occupied him during the day and night.

Late at night he'd look into the heavens,
And see three images with changing brightness.
At first their brightness would look just the same.

Two of them would be in the western skies,
And they would not steal each other's energies.
The third one would shine in the eastern skies,
And that one always would be trying to rob
The energies of the other two bodies.

Chalax couldn't grasp the sense of these visions.
He started to meditate day and night.
He then realized that these visions were
Standing for the Indians and the White Men.

Those two fainter spheres in the west stood for
The Blackfeet and the Pend Oreille people.
They could neither outshine nor disappear.

The sphere with the bright lights in the eastern
Skies stood for the White Men on the move.

A Break From the Visions

Chalax looked beyond the visions to be
Sure that not only mothers but also
The entire clan kept an eye on the children,
For a loving mood feeds the children's souls.

Grandparents ought to be the big landmark,
Like a rock at the junction of the paths of life,
So kids would know which path is the right one.

Would the parents realize that they are
Living in the lodges of their children?
So they're obliged to keep them welcoming.

After a terrifying night of nightmares,
What could be better than a restful sleep?

During a hot summer day on a trail,
When a mother quenches the thirst of her
Baby with her last swallow of water,
She will be quenching her own thirst as well.

A bashful mother, who may be as
Gentle as a cottontail, will turn as
Fierce as a sow while defending her young ones.

A caring mother grows invisible
Fuzz on her palms to make her touches softer.

A father, as courageous as an eagle,
Will turn as docile as a prairie chicken
While sheltering his chick under his wings.

It is easy to see how chicks can teach
Their parents how to savor life itself.

The Interpretation of the Chalax's Visions

An old man said, "We heard about your visions,
Just as secondhand information.
We could patronize you or ignore you,
For we have no direct information
Coming from your mouth to stop the hearsay."

Chalax said, "Before I would say something,
I wanted to be sure that my visions
Were not coming from the evil spirits
To cause restlessness and anxiety,
To the citizens of the Pend Oreilles."

"Now, I am sure that the spirits of our
Grandfathers are trying to alert us as
To what will happen and how it will affect us."

The two faint glows next to each other stand for
The peoples of Blackfeet and the Pend Oreilles.
They are more like each other than unlike.
We, the Pend Oreille people, fear and talk
About the raids of the Blackfeet people.

What happens if their raid is successful?
In a hurry Blackfeet Braves grab a couple
Of Pend Oreille girls to take with them to marry,
And a couple of healthy boys to raise
Them as their own and make them pathfinders.

The main issue over here is that they leave.
They don't prevent us from using our lands.

We continue to hunt the buffalo
From the same herd and catch the salmon from
The very same river, next to each other.
So we're alike with each other than unlike.

The Coming of the White Men

The bright celestial body stands for
The White Men who at the present landed on
Our eastern shores, and after catching their
Breath, they will expand to our western shores.

Physically we are more like each other.
Both of us have one heart and two kidneys.
However, their approach to life is unlike.

We gently tippy-toe on the Mother Earth,
And pick up what she wants to donate to us.
When we harvest and look back, we see nothing
Is disturbed and the Earth still stays the same.

When we need meat, then we hunt just enough
For our needs without hurting the whole herd.
As for the salmon, we catch what we need.
We've no silos or warehouses to fill.

White Men, disapprovingly, refer to
Our way of doing things as a "Hunter Gatherer
Economy" although it did work for us.

What brought Indians to their knees was not
The superior weapons of the White Men,
Or the pestilences they brought with them,
And exposed the Indians who had no

Immunity; many died but some survived.
And continued to do business as before.

When the Indian lands were occupied,
Parceled, privatized, fenced, and decorated
With no trespassing signs and Indians
Were confined in reservations,
And forced to live with other tribes with no
Prior relationship, Whites wanted to hear
One sentence from the civilized Indians,
"My noble Master, how may I serve you?"

In the reservation time goes slowly;
No digging, no picking, no tracking, no catching.

When Chalax finished his mission in this
Phase of his existence, he simply moved on.

Since he was a wild child and was adopted
And taken care of by the wild animals,
Both the hungry predatory animals,
And the creatures of the prey attended
The funeral, without bothering each other.

It was a day of forgetting ill wills,
And a day of celebrating the goodwill.
And a Blackfeet delegation was present.

The next day at sunrise, they transported the remains
Of Chalax to the Memaloose Island,
And left it on the purification boulder.
Wide Eyed Owl, touched the body which felt
As light as the body feathers of an eagle.

He balanced the body on his index
Finger and said, "As you can see, all I've
Is energy which does not need absolving.
So, the funeral is finished and over."

He waived towards a cedar which is prostrated
In front of the body, and the medicine man
Placed the body at the top branch of the cedar.
Then the cedar straightened itself up.

The True Identity of Selma Seeker

Selma said to Arpad, "The funeral
Of Chalax may be over; yet the story
Of the Pend Oreilles is still a mystery.
What is more, we do not know each other."
"When we met for the first time, I presented
Myself simply as a storyteller,
Which is truthful, though it is not the important
Part of my life and my accomplishments.

"There has to be a person in our tribe
Who's called the "keeper of the Sacred Sayings."
That soul may be a female or a male.

"I'm the last keeper of the Sacred Sayings.
To be a keeper, one has to be chosen
By the elders when babies give their first smile.

"Once a baby is chosen, her lifelong
Education starts and continues
All through her life without interruptions.

"The keeper can't add or delete a word.
Each verse has a matching sketch on a rawhide.

"I'm the last keeper of the Sacred Sayings.
So it's my responsibility to
Find a person to give the rawhides to.

"We cannot ask from ourselves more than
What we have been taught and what we believe.

"It is said that for the brighter new days
To come, we must lose everything we have.

"Since you were not chosen and educated
By the elders, you can't be the spiritual
Keeper of the sacred sayings, but you
Can safeguard them until a chosen one
Would come and claim my tapes and the sketchings.

"We can't choose everything but we're chosen
To do certain tasks for we have the gift.

"Since you're a White Man, you think that you've found me.
Actually I allured you for you have
Abilities that I can put to use.

"I know that you are an expert reader
Of runic inscriptions and a careful
Interpreter of ancient cave drawings.

"You have translated Turkish Ergenekon inscriptions
Into a modern Hungarian dialect.

"I will chant the sayings in Pend Oreilles,
Then chant them in English when I am
Pleased with the accuracy of the verse,
I will record it in both languages.

"It was said that we Indians must lose everything,
And darkness must fall upon us,
Before we can be awakened to see
The pure light and live in it forever.

"When I finish the chanting, you will find
A matching drawing on the deer rawhides."

They stayed at the Spokane House and for days
And nights, Selma recited the sacred
Sayings, both in English and in Pend Oreille.
When she was satisfied with the accuracy.
She made copies in both languages.

Then she asked to be driven to her home.
From then on, Konyas lost contact with her.

They remember her as the one who'd hear
The silence and see the invisible.

Sunka Khuciyela

Sacred Sayings of the Pend Oreille Elders

There was an era where there was nothing but God,
At His own time, He took an insignificant
Piece from himself and by utilizing that piece,
He created these infinite Universes.

As we judge now, life and death, light and darkness,
Warmth and coldness, likeness and unlikeness,
The matter and space were all together.

The nature of the Great Spirit is beyond
The comprehension of human beings.
He has no beginning nor ending.
He is an existence without any needs.

He evenly mixed the nonexistence
With the empty space and rubbed them together
To build a fierce fire, and the cinders of that
Fire became this Immense Universe.
He kept the Sun and the Stars burning so that
They could supply heat and light for the Earth.
Also in due time, He cooled down the Earth,
Cushioned it with the air and soaked it with
Fresh water and then sowed the seeds of life.

Life flourished behind the thousands of masks;
Yet Grandfathers kept track of their children.
They can observe us under any guise.

Grandfathers are the fish which swim and spawn
In the lake, or the grizzly who stands tall,
Or the pine which shoots toward the skies, or
The grass which lies under your moccasins.

As the life matured and learned to explore
The unbeaten paths, some were satisfied
With mere life itself. They stayed near the roots;
For others, the journey itself was the life.

When our ancestors settled at the shores
Of the Lake Pend Oreille, the Sun and the Moon
Were younger; as they grew older they've changed,
For the change is an unchangeable law.
From the start, the ancestors observed that all
Forms of lives journey on four legs which are
Made available to all without any
Favoritism: Earth, air, sun and water.

And each form of life travels on another
Form of life; if the grass were to lose one
Of her legs and stop growing, it will

Cripple all of her brothers and sisters.
Grandfathers grew wiser by harmonizing
With the basic harmony of this world.
They conversed with the spirit of their prey,
For one to live another one must die.

They've walked on Earth without leaving footprints.
As they've satisfied their hunger, they never
Asked for more than the Earth could provide for
They'd see the needs of those yet to be born.

In time, even Grandfathers were infested
With plague of self pride which plugged their ears,
So they could not hear the old guiding words.

They persuaded themselves that they were not
A part of the whole, but the whole itself.

Whatever we may say about God with human
Language won't apply to the Infinite Being.

There may be an individual relationship
With God which turns into perfect love or heartbreak.

Nothing in this Universe can be wholly
Vile for their souls directly come from God.

When one dies his body goes back to the Earth,
Although his soul lives on by joining God.

There is nothing like Hell for all things have
Some God given substance; would God burn Himself?

We cannot comprehend how heavenly
Shall be the Heaven, so we cannot give
Advice as to how you should act? when you
Meet with God, all we can say search your soul.

Your inner voice may sound in a way that,
It may not be the best advice, still follow
It without being sure that it will help.

We ought to yearn for a life style that is
Peaceful and intimate with Mother Earth.

Whether we classify them as inanimate
Or animate, everything came from the same source.
No new force can make the parts of the whole unclean,
Since the source of everything is Unadulterated.

Help comes to us in multiple ways,
Everything in this Universe is changing
By means of constant demise and rebirth.

A keen eye can see the truth in all places;
Religion is a human self-expression.
God is not in need of a religion.

God does not choose one faith over the other;
He blesses them all and love them equally.

If you like to be close to someone or
Something who's close to God; Kiss your own hand.

Do not worry about the events that
Have their build in natural solutions.
Do you have the smarts to recognize them?
Do you have the patience to wait and see them?

In this Universe nothing is too big
To be more important due to its size.

A stampeding buffalo herd's hoof beats
Would shake the ground for a short passing moments.

Soon after that the dust would settle and
The grass will grow as if nothing has happened.

During a dark night, a black ant's hip joint's
Pain shall be noticed and help shall be given.

No help shall be denied on the basis
Of the size of any living creature.

Help comes to us in myriad of ways.
Wait and see the natural solutions.

Every face comes with two similar sides.
We like to show the most beautiful side.

We must know the dark sides and embrace them
So that, we can keep them under control.

Everything in this universe is changing,
Yet many things can take care of themselves.
Don't tackle the things that could take care of themselves.

Our culture is urging us to remember
As to what has happened during the past wars.
This approach did not prevent any war;
It only kept the fires of wars smoldering.

We say," Forget the Trojan Wars. Forget
The Ergenekon Legends. And forget
The World War I. forget the World War II,
And don't forget to forget the Alamo.

In the contest of wars there are no winners.
Having better weaponry is no help,
For the other side can build better weapons.

God gave to human being the gift of speech,
And the first uttered words were "Love and Peace."
Along the way the word of "War" somehow
Infiltrated into the common language.

The most forgettable word should be "War,"
Yet we keep the memories of wars alive.

There is no unstoppable juggernaut;
There is nothing like final victory.
Nothing is permanent; in time weaker
Grows stronger, and the strong grows weaker.

Mass killings did not end with the Holocaust.
In Srebrenica Moslem males were slaughtered.
To come clean, we have to forgive and forget.
Don't let the history repeat itself.

When doubt arises, know that it, too,
Will fall away; sit with it; do nothing;
For you are nothing in this universe.
You're born to die; enjoy while you're alive.

Provincial people's altruism always
Triumphs over their sleeping egotism,
Though tranquility won't draw folk's attention.
Speak no evil, and mention no names of wars.

The war shows its true self during the post-war years.
The Blackfeet folks pull back and let us live our lives,
Whereas once the White Men put their feet on our lands,
They did not go back and we were not free.

The war promoters talk about preventing
The world from the forces of tyranny.
The only force that is available to prevent
The tyranny is the weaponless peace.

Animosities and separatism
Are not conditions that we are born with.

Some people live and remember after
The wars; and yet, only by forgetting
The wars, a peaceful world can be cemented.
The war tales should never be in schoolbooks;
And the war related weaponry should
Never be welcomed in the museums.

While judging yourself do not dig too deep
For God will provide you a restful sleep.

We went the distance with ordinary people;
Then we went the same distance with chosen people.

Now each one of us is walking the distance: Lone.

Printed in the United States
By Bookmasters